When I Was Young

A WARTIME CHILDHOOD

Rebecca Hunter with Angela Downey

Evans

First published in this edition in 2012 by Evans Brothers Ltd
2A Portman Mansions
Chiltern St
London W1U 6NR

www.evansbooks.co.uk

British Cataloguing in Publication Data

Hunter, Rebecca, 1935-
A wartime childhood. — (When I was young)
1. World War, 1939-1945—Social aspects—Great Britain—
Juvenile literature. 2. Great Britain—Social life and
customs—1918-1945—Juvenile literature.
I. Title II. Series III. Downey, Angela.
941'.084-dc22

ISBN-13: 9780237543846

Acknowledgements
Planning and production by Discovery Books Limited
Edited by Rebecca Hunter
Commissioned photography by Alex Ramsay
Designed by Calcium

The publisher would like to thank Angela Downey for her kind help in the preparation of this book.

For permission to reproduce copyright material, the author and publishers gratefully acknowledge the following: The Advertising Archive Limited: 23 (bottom); AKG London: 10 (top); London Borough of Wandsworth: 19 (bottom); Hulton Getty: 10 (bottom), 25, 26; The Imperial War Museum: 8 (bottom), 9 (top), 13 (top), 15, 16, 17, 19 (top), 20, 22, 23 (top), 24; The London Borough of Lambeth Archives Department: 7; Peter Newark's Pictures: 11, 12, 18 (bottom); The Robert Opie Collection: cover, 8 (top).

Contents

'I was born in 1937'

My name is Angela, and today I'm telling my family about my childhood during the **Second World War**. This is Adam who is thirteen, Jack who is eleven and Luke who is five.

When I was young, my family lived in Clapham, London. The picture above shows what Clapham looked like when I was young.

My dad worked for the post office and my mum was a housewife. I had two older brothers called Cecil and John.

I was born in 1937 before the Second World War. Many things changed after the war started. I am going to tell you about what life was like during the war.

'We all had gas masks.'

The war started in Europe in 1939. We were all given rubber gas masks in case poison gas was dropped from aeroplanes. Children's gas masks were made in bright colours to make them less frightening.

THIS SPECIAL RESPIRATOR FOR SMALL CHILD IS GOVERNMENT PROPERTY. ANY PERSON WHO HAS IT IN HIS POSSESSION IS RESPONSIBLE IN LAW FOR USING CARE TO KEEP IT IN GOOD CONDITION. IT IS TO BE RETURNED TO THE LOCAL AUTHORITY IN WHOSE AREA THE POSSESSOR MAY BE AT ANY TIME, EITHER ON REQUEST OR WHEN NO LONGER REQUIRED.

It was very dangerous living in London. Air-raid sirens made a terrible wailing noise when the enemy planes were coming to drop bombs. You had to find shelter quickly.

Some of our neighbours built **Anderson bomb shelters** like this in their gardens, but we sheltered in Clapham Common underground station.

Small children were put in siren suits to keep them warm in the shelters. This is me wearing one.

'Put out that light!'

Air raids took place at night. My brothers helped my mum put up big black curtains over the windows so enemy planes couldn't see the lights from our house.

ARP wardens walked up and down our street checking that no light could be seen outside. If they saw even a chink of light through the curtains they shouted, 'Put out that light!'

The picture on the left shows a warden's post made out of sandbags. Sandbags were used as protection during air raids.

It was dangerous to be outside during the **blackout** because there were no street lights and cars drove about without lights on.

White lines were painted on kerbs and steps to help people find their way, but there were still lots of accidents.

Pat Keely

UNTIL YOUR EYES GET USED TO THE DARKNESS, TAKE IT EASY

LOOK OUT IN THE BLACKOUT

'I was evacuated to Devon.'

In 1940 my father was **called up** and sent with the army to fight abroad. The government said that children in cities should be **evacuated** to the countryside, which was safer.

LEAVE THIS TO US SONNY—<u>YOU</u> OUGHT TO BE OUT OF LONDON

MINISTRY OF HEALTH EVACUATION SCHEME

My two brothers were sent to Yorkshire. I was evacuated in 1941 to a small village in Devon called Clyst St Mary. My mum came with me.

The train was packed with other children. We all had labels around our necks with our names, ages and where we were going. We carried our gas masks in a box strung around our necks. I took my favourite doll with me too, in case she got broken in the bombing.

'I went to the local school.'

When we got to Clyst St Mary I met the family who were going to **foster** me and said goodbye to my mum. I would see her only once a year for the next three years. I felt very homesick.

This is how Clyst St Mary looked then. It was very quiet compared to London.

I went to the local village school. The school kept daily records of events. Here are the records for two weeks in March 1942 showing the arrival of an evacuee and the dates when the gas masks were checked.

Exeter was our nearest big town. Sometimes I went shopping there with my foster mum.

'Everyone joined in with war work.'

Life was hard for everyone during the war. Many men had to leave their jobs and families to join the armed forces. Others did war work in factories. My foster dad worked in a factory in Exeter, building and repairing aircraft.

Any men who were not involved in the fighting were encouraged to help in the war effort by joining the **Local Defence Volunteers**.

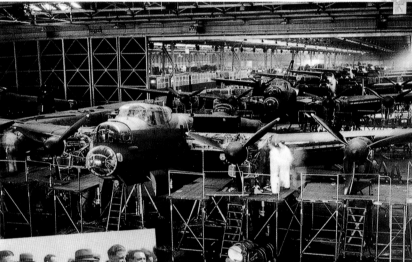

To start with they had no uniforms or weapons. They looked quite funny parading in their ordinary clothes with broom handles instead of rifles!

The boy scouts in our village used to collect **salvage**. Old saucepans, kettles, tin cans and iron railings could be made into new war weapons.

Farmers still needed help to grow food on the farm so women were encouraged to join the Women's Land Army. Many young women came down to the countryside to work on the farms.

'London was bombed in the Blitz.'

My mum had stayed in London to work as a ticket collector for London Transport.

Enjoy your Way Work

Look out in the blackout

GOOD PAY · FREE UNIFORM AND AN INTERESTING JOB

LONDON NEEDS MORE WOMEN BUS AND TRAM CONDUCTORS

SEE LARGE POSTERS FOR PARTICULARS

She sent me letters telling me how hard life was in London. She told me food was in very short supply because ships carrying supplies could not get through.

Many foods were **rationed**. Everyone had a ration book with coupons showing how much they could buy all week.

People were encouraged to grow their own vegetables. Clapham Common (above), where we used to play, was turned into allotments!

Many areas in London were badly damaged by the **Blitz**. This is Balham High Road after a bombing raid.

'We played in the fields.'

Life in Devon was easier than in London. Although food was rationed we ate quite well. I helped my foster dad in the garden where we grew our own vegetables. Country life was a new experience for me and I enjoyed visiting a farm for the first time and playing in the fields at hay-making time.

In 1942 I heard that my dad had been killed fighting overseas. I hadn't seen him for two years and now I would never see him again.

This made me very worried about my mum. Here is a letter I sent her telling her what I was doing and how I felt. I called myself Ann when I was a child.

Clyst St Mary

My Dea Mum
　　　　Here is a line
hoping you are a Lot
BettER And will be
out of Hospital soon
I have A new school
Teacher I have been
good At school and
never Had the cane
once I went in Exeber
Last Thursday with
Pegg and gwen To
get a pair of Sand
als give My Love to
Cecil ALL MYLove
MuMy. God BLess you
and keep you from the
bombs Love Ann

'We loved the American soldiers.'

Parachutes and **armaments** were made in Exeter. This made the city a target for enemy attack. In 1942 the city was badly bombed. The boards in this picture show where the shops used to stand. Fortunately the cathedral was not damaged.

America was one of our **allies** in the war and many American soldiers arrived in the country to help fight. The boys in our village loved to talk to them and try on their uniforms.

Everyone loved the American soldiers because they could get things like chocolate and cigarettes that were in short supply. They would drive through the village in their trucks, throwing sweets and chewing gum out of the windows to the children.
I had never tasted chewing gum before!

'I returned home for Christmas.'

My brothers and I finally returned home to London in time for Christmas 1944, shortly before the war ended.

London had been badly hit by a new type of flying bomb – the V1, or doodlebug. It made a droning noise as it travelled. When the noise stopped, you knew the bomb was dropping down to explode.

This picture shows Clapham after it was hit by a doodlebug.

Later came an even more terrifying weapon – the V2 rocket – which gave no warning at all. You couldn't hear them coming until it was too late. This picture shows one, about to be launched on London.

My brothers and I enjoyed playing on bomb sites. We made dens and hiding places in ruins and searched for pieces of **shrapnel** amongst the rubble. I broke my arm falling off a homemade swing.

'Parties went on for days.'

The war in Europe finally ended in May 1945, although the war against Japan went on until August. Victory in Europe, or VE Day as it became known, was declared and we all celebrated.

DAILY EXPRESS

WAR OVER IN GERMANY, HOLLAND AND DENMARK

GERMANS SURRENDER INSIDE MONTY'S TENT

They argued, they wept, they went and lunched— but said 'Yes' at last

THE MAP CONVINCED THEM

Street parties, with bonfires, fireworks and music went on all over the country for many days. The local council gave a party in our school to celebrate. There were many decorations and flags, and food like jelly and ice cream that we hadn't tasted for a very long time.

Here is a photo of that party. I am sitting on the right.

'After the war.'

Last year I returned to the village of Clyst St Mary to show my husband where I had spent most of the war.

A lady in the village found this photograph showing me (holding the dog) which was taken after the war had finished.

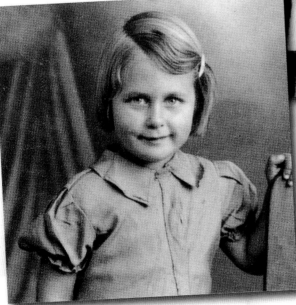

I lived through some exciting times during the war but I will never forget how many people lost their lives. I certainly wouldn't want my family to live through a war like that.

Glossary

Air raids Attacks from the air by aeroplanes, rockets and bombs.

Allies Britain, the USA and the USSR fought together as allies against Germany, Italy and Japan.

Anderson shelter An outdoor air raid shelter made of corrugated steel.

Armaments Military weapons and equipment.

ARP wardens Air Raid Precautions (ARP) wardens were responsible for checking air raid shelters and enforcing the blackout.

Blackout Making sure no light was visible from houses or streets so that towns were invisible from the air.

Blitz The 'Blitzkrieg' or 'Blitz' was the heavy night-time bombing of British cities in 1940 and 1941.

Call up An order from the government to join the armed forces.

Evacuate To remove people from a dangerous place to a safer one.

Foster to look after children that were not your own.

Local Defence Volunteers A voluntary group of men who wanted to help defend their towns and villages if there was an attack.

Rationing Limiting the amount of food and clothing that a person is allowed to buy.

Salvage To re-use goods and materials for other purposes.

Second World War A war fought around the world between 1939 and 1945. Germany, Italy, Japan and their allies were on one side and Britain, the United States, the Soviet Union and their allies were on the other.

Shrapnel Small fragments of bombs.

Useful books and websites

There are lots of books to read and websites to visit to learn more about wartime childhood. Here are a few to get you started:

http://www.iwm.org.uk/upload/package/20/lifeinww2/children/childindex.htm
Learn about life for children during the Second World War.

http://www.bbc.co.uk/schools/primaryhistory/world_war2/
A BBC site with lots of facts, activities and quizzes about life during the Second World War.

http://www.nationalarchives.gov.uk/education/homefront/
Information about the Home Front.

At Home in World War Two series, Stewart Ross, Evans 2007
Dear Mum, I miss you (Flashbacks), Stewart Ross, Evans 2006
In the War series, various authors, Wayland 2008
What if the bomb goes off? (Flashbacks), Stewart Ross, Evans 2008

Activities and cross-curricular work

Activities suggested on this page support progression in learning by consolidating and developing ideas from the book and helping the children to link the new concepts with their own experiences. Making these links is crucial in helping young children to engage with learning and to become lifelong learners.

Ideas on the next page develop essential skills for learning by suggesting ways of making links across the curriculum and in particular to literacy, numeracy and ICT.

Word Panel

Check that the children know the meaning of each of these words and ideas from the book, in addition to the words in the glossary.

- Abroad
- Afterwards
- Ago
- Air-raid siren
- Allotments
- Before
- Enemy
- Poison gas
- Sandbag
- Shelter
- Supplies
- War work
- Woman's land army

Research Questions

Once you have read and discussed the book, ask groups of children to talk together and think of more information they would like to know. Can they suggest where to look for the answers?

The Second World War

Find out more about the war. Let groups of children research different aspects and prepare talks for the rest of the class. Topics children could cover include:

- Geography – how global was the war? Which countries were involved?
- History – what had happened before the war?
- Weapons – for the army, navy or air-force
- The war on land, at sea or in the air
- The axis and the allies – who's who
- What happened to the wounded?
- The women's land army
- Evacuee children
- London during the Blitz
- Living in local towns and cities.

Posters and Propaganda

Talk about why the government would want to communicate with the people during the war. Remind children that there was no internet and very few families had TV. The government could communicate through newsreels in cinemas, the wireless radio, leaflets and posters.

- Find contemporary propaganda material in libraries and online and evaluate it.
- Research other accounts of what was happening at the same time in the war. Did the propaganda material tell the same story? Talk about why and why not.
- Listen to the language of broadcast media. Identify words which show that it's morale building rather than necessarily the entire truth.
- Talk about how access to the internet might change a future war.

VE celebration

Prepare your classroom for a VE celebration:
- Research the music of the times so you have appropriate sounds.
- Research what kinds of party foods could be made using rationed foods: look for wartime cook books and try making some of the foods.
- Make union flags to decorate.
- Make bunting from old scraps of fabric.
- Play party games.

Using 'A Wartime Childhood' for cross-curricular work

The web below indicates some areas for cross-curricular study. Others may well come from your own class's engagement with the ideas in the book.

The activities suggested will help children to develop key competencies as:

- successful learners
- confident individuals and
- responsible citizens.

Cross-curricular work is particularly beneficial in developing the thinking and learning skills that contribute to building these competencies because it encourages children to make links, to transfer learning skills and to apply knowledge from one context to another. As importantly, cross-curricular work can help children to understand how school work links to their daily lives. For many children, this is a key motivation in becoming a learner.

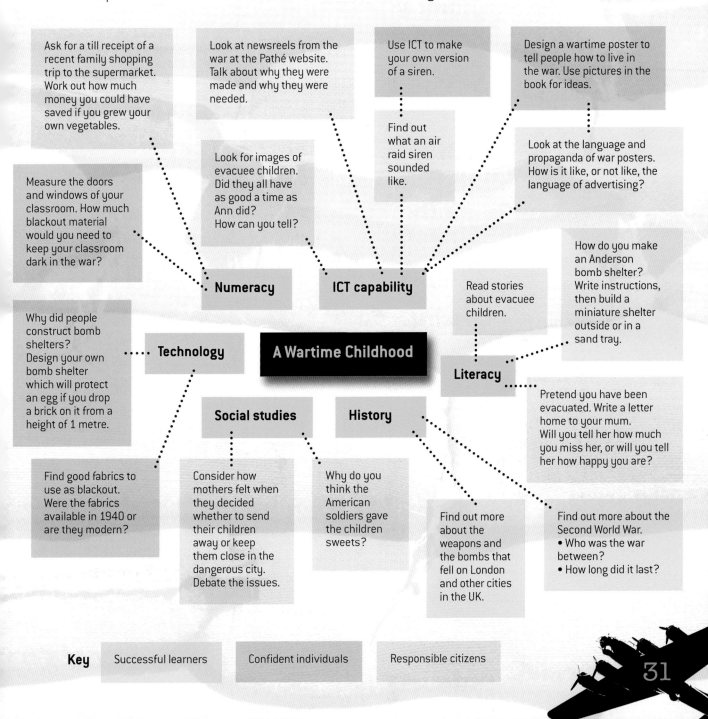

Ask for a till receipt of a recent family shopping trip to the supermarket. Work out how much money you could have saved if you grew your own vegetables.

Look at newsreels from the war at the Pathé website. Talk about why they were made and why they were needed.

Use ICT to make your own version of a siren.

Design a wartime poster to tell people how to live in the war. Use pictures in the book for ideas.

Find out what an air raid siren sounded like.

Look for images of evacuee children. Did they all have as good a time as Ann did? How can you tell?

Look at the language and propaganda of war posters. How is it like, or not like, the language of advertising?

Measure the doors and windows of your classroom. How much blackout material would you need to keep your classroom dark in the war?

How do you make an Anderson bomb shelter? Write instructions, then build a miniature shelter outside or in a sand tray.

Numeracy

ICT capability

Read stories about evacuee children.

Why did people construct bomb shelters? Design your own bomb shelter which will protect an egg if you drop a brick on it from a height of 1 metre.

Technology

A Wartime Childhood

Literacy

Pretend you have been evacuated. Write a letter home to your mum. Will you tell her how much you miss her, or will you tell her how happy you are?

Social studies

History

Find good fabrics to use as blackout. Were the fabrics available in 1940 or are they modern?

Consider how mothers felt when they decided whether to send their children away or keep them close in the dangerous city. Debate the issues.

Why do you think the American soldiers gave the children sweets?

Find out more about the weapons and the bombs that fell on London and other cities in the UK.

Find out more about the Second World War.
- Who was the war between?
- How long did it last?

Key   Successful learners   Confident individuals   Responsible citizens

31

Index